MORNING ROUTINES OF THE RICH AND FAMOUS

ANALYZING THE SUCCESSFUL TO BECOME SUCCESSFUL

Description

This great book focuses on all the things that the most successful and famous people in the world do in the morning to have a fruitful and fantastic day. You realize that there are many people who wake up very early in the morning but very few know what they must do to start a bright morning. It includes everything they must do from the time they get up from their beds, take their breakfasts, exercise, set their goals, check their emails and kiss their loved ones good bye and then leave for work. The book does not just talk about morning passions and obsessions but it also includes an in-depth analysis of every little thing that celebrities, presidents, the wealthy and the well-to-do entrepreneurs do before they leave their homes in the morning. The morning routines highlighted on this book will help you learn all the rituals that you must adopt to become more successful.

Table of Contents

Introduction

A proper morning routine is what you need to achieve your goals and close the gap between you and the world's most successful people. Paying close attention to what they do from the time they wake up to the time they exit the door can help you to learn what you have been missing and what you should think of including in your day to day life. This is to help you get what you have always wanted. Waking up early at 4:00am or 3:00am is not enough. You need to learn to do more for you to be a successful and accomplished person. This book is for any person who feels they have not been doing things right in the morning. If you have been searching for the things you need to do in the morning to achieve your objectives then you should search no more.

All the successful morning routines highlighted on this book will help you focus on what you need to do during the day before something else comes along and shifts your attention. As you will realize from the routines listed on this book, switching off your Smartphone or PC connection is important to avoid interruptions during this important part of your day. Keep reading to know what you need to do in the morning for a healthy, wise and wealthy routine experience. Some of the most important things that you must include in your morning routine include drinking lemon water, sparing a few minutes for meditation, work outs, positive visualizations of goals, a sumptuous breakfast and proper personal hygiene.

What Is A Successful Morning Routine?

This is the question that you must find answers to even before you think of doing anything in the morning. Always remember that it's essential for you to start every morning on the right foot, doing what is right at the right time. If your morning is fabulous then you can take this perfection into the rest of your day with a positive mind ready to do your best.

Successful living is about being more realistic and positive in whatever you decide to do. A proper morning routine will help turn your mornings into the best time to feel relaxed, motivated, productive and optimistic to approach the rest of the day with confidence. Most successful people will walk out of their doors feeling energized, fast and ready to tackle all the challenges that come their way.

Things To Consider Before Designing A Successful Morning Routine

How much time can you spare?

Most people get off on the wrong foot by trying to optimize their morning routines by packing them with as many activities as possible. Actually, filling your morning routine with unreasonable targets is a sure way for you to fail miserably.

If you are supposed to be at your work place by 8:00am, it is much better for you to design a three-hour morning routine if you are able and ready to wake up at 5:00am. Otherwise, you should design a morning routine with the exact number of hours that you can afford to spare. Start by figuring out the total amount of time that you can afford to commit to your morning routine.

Can you advance the goals you have set via a successful morning routine?

Check out the goals that are more suited for an early morning routine than others. A goal of shedding 30 pounds can be achieved through morning routines but it would be unrealistic for you to think that you can become the proud owner of the largest oil company in the world through morning routines. Make sure that the only goals you have integrated in your morning routines are achievable or else you should find a way of tying the morning goals to your day to day haphazard actions.

Can you design a morning routine to suit your needs?

For instance, it will be useless for you to set an exercise morning routine in a gym that opens at 8:00am, when you are supposed to be busy in the office. It's impossible for you to be working out at the gym and planning your day's work at the office. Such an exercise will be more appropriate for people who have a home gym and can work at home during the rest of the day because they have the flexibility of hitting the gym at any time they want without any limitations. Either way, you should find the best way of getting started in the morning as you work your way up the ladder.

How To Get Started With The Best Morning Routine

The simple fact that you are here means that you have decided all the things that you want to include in your morning routine and you have already allocated the time you need. We strongly recommend that you spare at least three hours for a successful and fruitful morning routine.

There are a few reasons why getting started with the successful peoples' morning routine can be hard, but check out the best routines right here to get the most out of your morning hours.

1. **Wake up earlier than you did yesterday.**

When have you been waking up? After designing your daily morning routine, you will realize how later you have been waking up. At this point you should make a decision to wake up earlier so that you can get up much earlier than you used to. Start by rising up earlier in small bits, 20 – 40 minutes earlier, rather than just jumping to 3 hours at once. Consider going to bed much earlier than you used to in the past. You can also consider getting some tips for waking up early from different sources if desired.

2. **Consider your caffeine intake.**

At times, caffeine can be addictive. This is especially if you are not careful with how and when you take it in the morning. Swap that cup of coffee with something healthier and nutritious such as lemon, water or any other type of juice. Check out the most successful people and you will notice that they don't take coffee in the morning. Instead, most of them take green tea (it only has a bit of caffeine), which has many more health benefits than coffee.

What Is Success?

Different individuals think of success at a personal level. What you think about of success is not what the other person thinks about as being successful. If you ever want to be a successful person, the first thing that you should be concerned about is what success means to you regardless of what it means to other people. In most cases society defines a successful person as someone who has lots of money and can buy whatever they want, but that is not the case because a large number of the successful people as the society like calling them are not happy with their lives. Understanding what success is and being able to set your goals appropriately is the only way you can bring some meaning to the definition of success.

How To Make Your Morning Super Productive?

You can make your day to day life more profitable and productive by waking up every morning and setting your priorities right. Great morning routines are what makes successful people happier and gives them the motivation they require to go out there and make more money. First, they understand that their priorities come first than what other people hold; they don't consider what other people think in regard to what they do. Upon getting up every morning, the highly successful people out there do not just check their mail. To become a successful person, you must have the notion that your priorities come first no matter what. Keep reading to know what the rich and the famous do every morning when they wake up.

How Becoming A Morning Person Can Change Your Life

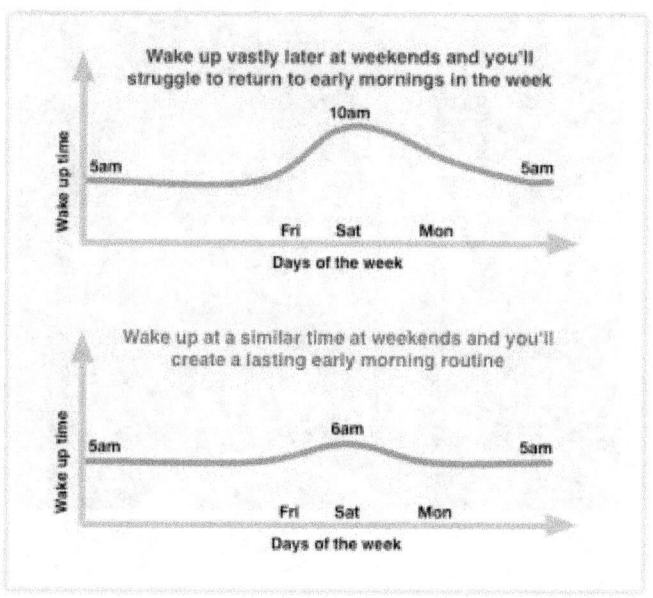

The secret to becoming a successful person is waking up early in the morning, hitting the gym, eating healthy and feeling motivated. The best people in the world have found a way of overcoming the morning blues; you will find them doing a whole lot more in the morning than most other people. Successful people wake up very early in the morning when others are still snoring or hitting the snooze button so that they can continue sleeping. Just as you are busy between the sheets, the rich and famous are busy with their lives, trying to find new ideas and working on the newest projects. Professional footballers, athletes, celebrities and entrepreneurs have a unique way of dealing with what they do best in the morning.

If you live on the same neighborhood with a successful person, you will realize how early they rise to start working out and practicing. Rising early in the morning can set you apart with your competition in the industry of value to you.

What Time Do Successful People Wake Up?

Just ask any CEO you meet about what time they wake up and you will be surprised with the answers that you get. Most of the executives managing top notch companies wake up as early as 3am. Usually, top executives wake up very early in the morning before their competitors to make their way into the office before anyone else. As a matter of fact, the best CEOs get to the office hours earlier than their colleagues. However, as the rich will tell you, the time that you rise up is not as important as what you have planned to do when you get up. The most important thing about waking up early is time management and ensuring that you make the most out of your morning hours.

What Do the Rich Do Every Morning?

Are you wondering what the rich and famous do every morning after they wake up? Worry no more; you just have to reschedule what you need to do every morning to fit into the class of the rich and successful.

Have you been feeling that you don't have enough time to do all your morning chores before you leave the house? Then you should probably consider waking up one hour earlier like the rich do so that you can have all the time you need to do all you need to do before leaving for work.

Successful people write down all the things they want to do the next morning, the night before they fall asleep. This way they will get up in the morning knowing exactly what they want to achieve.

Successful people design simple and effective morning routines and do their best to stick to them. The wealthy understand that every decision they make is determined by their mental health and that's why they want to make simple decisions in the morning when they are feeling fresh and energetic.

Important Morning Routine Suggestions

Wake Up Very Early

There is no doubt that time is a very important factor to the rich and famous. Highly successful and famous people wake up at 4:30am or 5:00am to make sure that they have total control over the morning hours.

Waking up early gives the most successful people the time they need to do what they have to do before they head to the office or start working from home. While it may be hard for you to adjust automatically, you can get started by waking up 20 minutes earlier than usual and then gradually set your time.

Waking up early will help you to avoid unnecessary headaches, tickets and tardiness. As a matter of fact, most businesses and offices open their doors by 9 o'clock. Regardless of whether you travel to an office or you work from home, the earlier you wake up, the better it will be for you because it helps you to beat competition. Make it trend to rise up earlier than other people so that you can get the best in life. Just as the saying goes," the early bird catches the worm."

Eat a Sumptuous Breakfast

The wealthy have a way of ensuring that they are healthy and have the energy required to keep going. As a matter of fact, the most famous people often follow doctor-prescribed diets that they take part in every morning to make sure they are healthy. Your productivity during the day is based on what you take in the morning. The rich will take a healthy breakfast to ensure they have the energy needed to do what they do best. As you will notice regardless of what happens, the rich never skip their breakfasts.

Your physical appearance, body speed and brain function are a reflection of what you take in the morning. Keep away from things that slow you down and focus on taking the nutrients that provide you with the energy needed to give you more energy. Grains, fruits and proteins will provide you with all the much needed energy that you require to keep you going without slowing you down.

Try visiting a successful person in the morning and check out what they take in the morning. In most cases you will find a mixture of apple, orange and lemon juices among other healthy and filling things of use.

Water

Water is an important constituent of what the rich take every morning when they wake up. There is no doubt that you need water to get through the day without feeling exhausted and tired. In fact, it is recommended that you take at least 500mL of water everyday in the morning to get your day started.

Bathroom

This point about getting into the day goes without saying; nobody will want to sit at the same table with someone who stinks. Ask any successful person to tell you the time they take in the bathroom and almost all of them spend 20 to 30 minutes of their time to clean themselves up in the bathroom. Heading to the bathroom promotes good personal hygiene and gets you started on the right note.

Stretching

Even the slightest body movement is an indication that the day has started. Some people will prefer to head to the gym for some push-ups and exercises on the treadmill. A fast 10 minute walk on the treadmill is exactly what many successful people can do to ensure they get started with enough force and motivation.

Exercise Daily

Apart from the health benefits that come with engaging in it, regular exercise routines in the morning can increase brain functions and reduce stress levels. Developing a regular exercise habit every morning before breakfast is a great tactic of ensuring that you can carry on the rest of the day successfully. You will find some of the most successful people working out in the gym by 5:00am in the morning. If possible, you should head outside and walk for at least 20 minutes. Apart from the wide range of health benefits, exercising in the morning will boost your metabolism.

Most of the successful and rich people I have read about wake up early and head to the gym. Actually, you may not know whether exercising in the morning comes as a result of being rich or a way of getting richer. As a matter of fact it might be easier to hit the gym in the morning knowing that you have some millions in the bank than when you don't have anything. The most interesting thing is that while the rich head to the gym every morning, their companies are still growing.

One important thing that we must appreciate is that healthy people who head to the gym regularly rarely get sick and as a result they will be able to work for long hours and pay more attention to what they do than those people who consume high fat diets.

The greatest motivation that you should get from the richest people is that, despite their busy lives, new projects, numerous commitments and several day to day activities, they are still able to find time to visit the gym every morning and work out for at least 30 minutes before heading to the office.

Work Out

Apart from being healthy, researchers have proven that working out in the morning is an excellent way of preparing your body for the day's activities ahead. Jogging in the morning also limits your stress levels so that you can get started with the positive energy required to become a more productive person. The key to hitting the gym early in the morning is ensuring that you have the energy you need to keep going in the course of the day.

Setting Goals

The most successful people review their goals every morning so that they can remind themselves of what they must do before the end of the day. They will check out their journals or task management systems as they take their breakfasts to see what they were not able to accomplish in the previous day. With the right strategies in place, they have an idea of what they want to achieve in the long term and this way they can focus all their energy there.

What are the most important goals to you at the moment? You should design your schedules with regard to the goals you have set. Always keep in mind that time is the most important resource, and if not well-managed, you could be heading the wrong direction. Regardless of what you do, there is no way you will ever be able to work 25/8/366.

Review Your Day's Objective List

While you already have a list of the things you want to do, you should keep restructuring them, ensuring that you have all that you need to accomplish on that to-do list. This should give you the motivation you need to push ahead. If you manage your time well then you will be able to manage more than you could within the same timeframe.

Handle Personal Projects

The most famous and successful people in the management world have dedicated the better part of their mornings to tackling personal projects that they don't have time to handle during the day. Tackling personal assignments in the morning makes them happier, less worried and eventually prepares them for the day's events. This great enthusiasm is what drives them to achieve more success in every little thing they do at work.

Tackle the Most Challenging Projects

The morning is the best time to handle those challenging and sharp projects that are almost due. With this, you will realize that you are very fresh in the morning. This should give you the energy you require to handle all the sensitive projects that are lying on your to-do list. The famous people out there all tend to rise up early to tackle the high priority projects that they need to do when they are fresh. The morning hours are also the best because you can do all the work you have without interruptions by employees and co-workers.

Hug Your Partner & Kiss Your Kids Goodbye

It may sound obvious, but the highly successful people out there have good relationships with their families. Acknowledging your family, wife and children before heading to work can help you relax emotionally. This should allow you to focus on the upcoming events that you are trying to get into. The main reason why you should want to become successful is so that the people who are the closest to you in your life can also benefit.

The early morning has become the best time to catch up with the family and your better half; this is the best way of parting to start your day. Some successful people have created enough time in the morning to ensure that they see their kids off to school. According to the latest research, people who create time to be with their families in the morning are more successful during the day.

Network

Most CEOs describe their mornings as the only time they have to connect with other people, employees, extended family members, clients, associates, friends and new customers. Since they are busy during the day, the morning is the best time for any executive to sit down and meet with anyone who is an asset to the company.

Networking in the morning is important because it helps you connect with other people. You will then have the rest of the day to do your work without interruptions.

Read the News

You will never be able to have any impact on the world if you don't know what is happening in the first place. You can use your laptop or smartphone to access the breaking news in your state; this will also help you know the latest trends in the corporate world.

Familiarizing with what is happening in the world around you will help you approach your latest investments with caution. You can do this for understanding exactly what the right thing for you to do can be.

Check Out the Business Daily

Most CEOs will check out the daily business newspapers to know the latest prices of shares and how other companies are doing. Apart from helping people to gauge their own companies, they are able to know what they are doing wrong. For celebrities, checking out the latest news will help them to know about the newest fashions and what bloggers are saying about them.

Email

While some people may push their mail-checking times to the evening hours, checking out your emails in the morning before you do anything else can help you to plan the day ahead. You can set aside some minutes in the morning to skim through your email inbox and prioritize the most important mails that require your immediate attention.

At the same point, you can also peruse through the detailed emails as you take in your breakfast. This way you can use the rest of the day to act on the information you got from your email inbox.

Plan the Day Ahead

There might be many times when you feel rushed off when you get to work with a never-ending to-do list because you did not plan your day in the morning. Taking a few minutes to plan what you want to do during the day in the morning will not only help save time but it will help you have enough time to do more during the day. Set some timeframes and deadlines in the morning as they will help you to have an effective day.

Understand the Timing

The morning ritual starts when you take 16 ounces of water and ends when you start your first task of the day. Indeed, your daily morning rituals should not take much of your time; they should be short and effective.

Small Changes To Your Daily Morning Routine That Will Change Your Entire Day

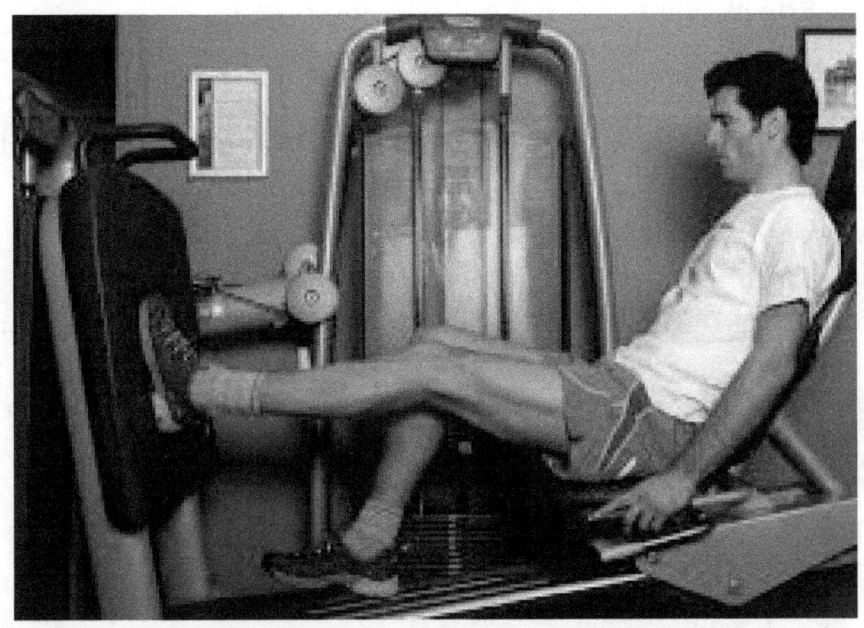

Better scheduling of your morning hours can set the right tone for productivity and positivity for the rest of the day. While setting your alarm clock to wake you up early in the morning can be beneficial, that is not enough. You need to plan how you are going to spend the first few minutes of your morning perfectly for excellent and the most successful results. Here is a look at how to can change your morning routine for the better as the rich do.

Avoid Screens

The first 20 minutes should be your time with no screens, no television, no smartphone and no alarm clock. Always make sure that your smartphone's email notifications have been switched off to avoid being tempted to check out the Facebook notifications and other things that may show up on your phone. Instead you should use the time to make proper plans for what you need to do during the rest of the day.

No Coffee Or Tea, Instead Go For Lemon Water

Instead of coffee, switch to a hot cup full of lemon water. It not only helps boost your metabolism but it also cleans your throat and provides you with the energy you need. It will not be a walk in the park for coffee addicts but it can be very beneficial to those who want to get the best out of their mornings. You are what you eat or drink and taking good care of your body will give you the physical capacity that you desperately need to complete all your needs and functions during the day.

Sit Up Properly

It may not be important to most people, but your sitting position when you wake up is important in making sure that you get up on the right tone. You should avoid getting up on your left side because it's not healthy. If possible you should get up on the right side of your bed; this way you will have started your morning right.

Set Reasonable Goals

Setting achievable goals for the day while taking your lemon water will help put your priorities right, knowing exactly what you need to do so that you can achieve your goals. Avoid setting unreasonable goals because they might discourage you in the future. This is not a thing that successful people do.

Meditate

It may seem obvious and stupid, but this is something that you might consider doing if you want to succeed in life. Meditating is a long, boring and strict session that most people think is of as waste of time that does not have any benefits whatsoever but that is not the case. In fact, you can even meditate for less than a minute.

On the other hand, sitting pretty in a comfortable position helps clear your mind and focus on what you need to do during the day. By now you already know the morning routines that you need to change so you can then embrace the new effective ones.

Exercise

As mentioned earlier, most of the people who work out every day often do so early in the morning. Whether it's walking on the treadmill or engaging in yoga, exercising in the morning helps boost your energy levels by boosting your metabolism. With this, you will have the right mood to forge ahead to your day to day accomplishments.

Working out in the morning helps you avoid the flakes that come into a gym after a long day at work. Some pushu-ps and body stretches will help prepare you for the busy day ahead. All you have to do is consult an expert in physiotherapy to know about the most appropriate exercises that you should participate in.

Perfect Morning Routines

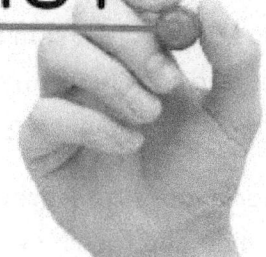

You can easily maximize your day's potential by mapping out your plans for the day and the objectives that you want to achieve at the end of the day. The morning hours are the best for a person to make plans for without any disruptions. In most cases the day is filled with busy schedules and the morning is the only time you can get the most suitable atmosphere for your working needs.

The best time for you to prioritize on what you what to do during the day is in the morning. If you have been feeling that everything is not fitting in with your day schedule then the morning hours will give you a chance to handle additional tasks that do not fit on your time table without interruptions. Never forget to take a few minutes for a short break as you take a walk or meditate on your desk so that you can get your priorities right. You can also pack a few snacks in your bag so that you can have something to eat when working in the office.

Eat Healthy

A cup of coffee and an empty stomach is the worst breakfast you can ever take if you ever even want to expect to have a wonderful day in the office. Imagine spending the first few hours in the office wondering when the snack truck or desk will come calling outside your office block. Instead, you should take a few minutes in the morning to fill up your stomach so you can have the energy required to handle the tasks ahead.

This will help you concentrate on what you need to do to become a successful person rather than just thinking about your growling stomach. Eating a healthy breakfast is not only good for your stomach but it's also excellent for your emotional connections. Sparing a few seconds to eat some oatmeal will prepare you mentally for whatever may come about before you walk out of the door.

Positive Visualization

Most of the time we pay more attention to our physical health and overlook our mental health, a point in life which is far more important. The first morning hours are the best to meditate and visualize inside your mind. Most of the rich people I know take a few minutes to visualize, focusing more on the successes that they can achieve during the day if they do their best; this helps them work extra harder so that they can achieve their objectives. You should avoid focusing on the negative energy that you are bearing with when visualizing because this could create some negative energies in your mind. Positive visualization in the morning will help you overlook your obstacles during the day.

4 Early Morning Rituals To Boost Your Spirits All Day Long

Most people work for eight hours a day or even more depending on the position one is in and the amount of responsibility that may come with it. Unfortunately, most of us are not able to handle all our daily schedules for the most part and as a result have to carry and bring our work home. This means that we have to complete the day's work at the expense of other things such as family relations and much more. here are the four most important things that you should incorporate in your morning schedule to help make the most out of your office time and boost your productivity.

1. **10 Minutes of Exercise**

You should not take more time to exercise than needed; just ten minutes of your morning time will not have any huge impact on your morning routine but it will shed off any sluggishness and boredom from the sheets and the few glasses of wine you had taken in the night before. While there are many fitness exercises that you can participate in, the 10 minute workout works perfectly when it comes to stretching your muscles. You can also talk with your fitness coach to know more about the easiest workouts that you can engage in while doing so in less than 10 minutes so you can save more time. Always remember that regular morning exercise helps you to get started with much more zeal and determination.

2. **Eat Some Greens**

Starting your day green with a green smoothie. It may not be as enticing as grabbing a cup of yogurt or reaching for a bowl of cereal but is much healthier and helps you save time. Unlike the bagel that you must take time to toast, juicing does not require much time. You should consider blending one apple, one orange, one banana and any other fruit that works for you. Juicing is not only less expensive but it's also easy to prepare and more energetic to the body.

3. **Catch Up With Your Partner**

While this is normally used as an evening conversation, you can as well have it in the morning before you leave the house. This involves discussing with your partner points about the few things that you want to achieve at the end of the day. Think of the three most important things that you want to achieve in the next 12 hours so that you can feel that the day was successful. Although this won't be a guarantee that you will achieve all you want to, it will keep the ball rolling.

4. **Choose Three Wins**

This includes highlighting the three most essential things you would be happy to achieve at the end of the day. The point of this step is to do all you can to ensure that the goals you have set are achievable. This is to help you avoid unnecessary stress by setting some unreasonable objectives.

Great And Effective Ways How Rich People Design Their Mornings

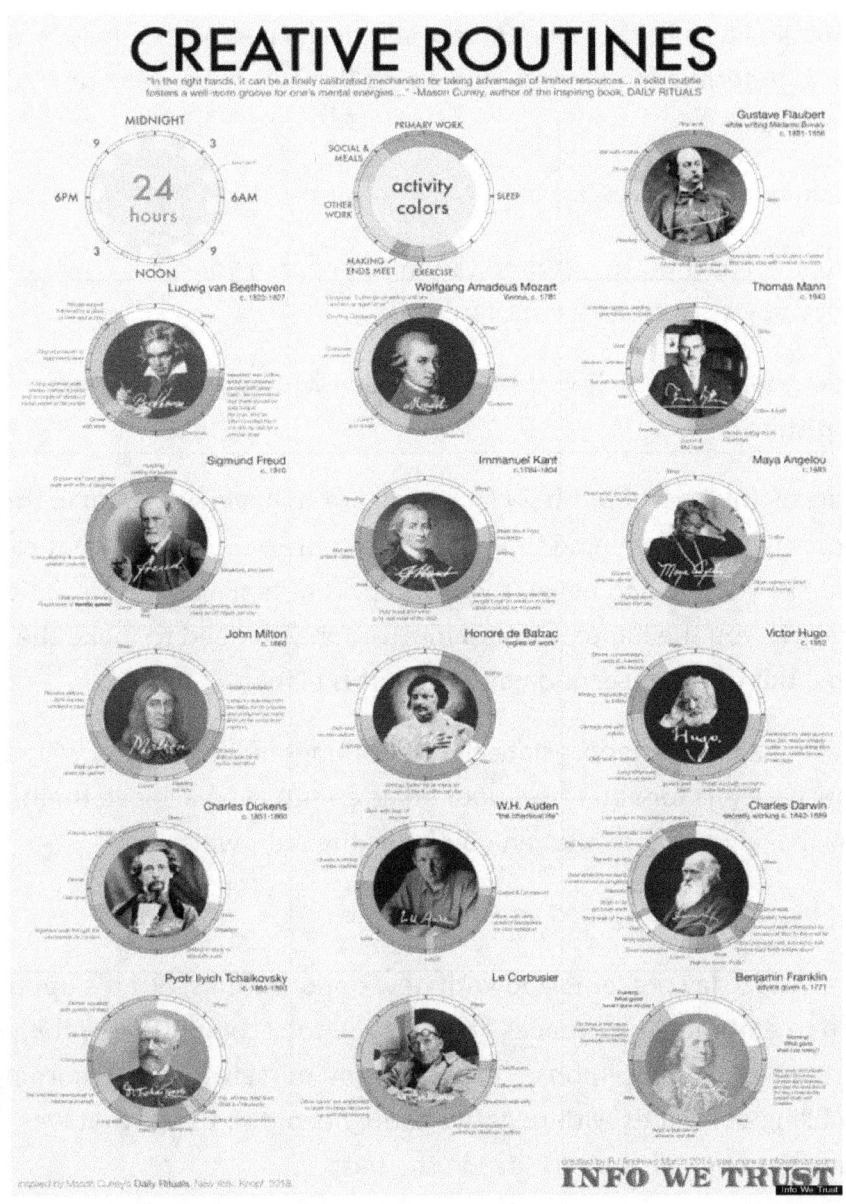

The early morning is very important because it's the foundation through which the rest of the day is built upon. Your morning routine can efficiently determine how the rest of your day is going to be and also if you going to be a successful person or a failure. All this is determined by the things we do first when we wake up in the morning.

Positive Meditation

You need to think about meditation to improve your life. There are a few points to consider in this case:

How good can it be if you start your day with grace, love and gratitude?

Start by thinking about how lucky you are to have woken up in the morning, having in mind that there are some people who went to bed like you did and haven't woken up. That feeling of appreciation will give you the happiness and motivation you need to make the most out of every second you live on this planet.

Make it a habit to appreciate the finer things in life and you will see how easy it is for you to set your goals and to even achieve them. It will make you happier when you focus the right way.

Let bygones be bygones and start a new.

Every new day presents you with new opportunities, but it's upon you to embrace the chances given to you to accomplish new things. Instead, most of us impose restrictions on ourselves in the morning by filling our minds with negative thoughts of the things that we have not been able to achieve in the past.

Why should you hold yourself hostage over the things that you were not able to achieve yesterday while you have been accorded a new chance to prove yourself? Every morning should be the best time for you to set your priorities right. Avoid silly mistakes that you made in the previous day and lost a few hours; let this be a new dawn for you to show what you are made of.

Live a morning as it comes.

You should live everyday as it comes and avoid pre-occupying yourself with negative energy. You should live your morning to the fullest. Why do all that you have been doing in the past today?

Consider embracing a few new things here and there for more success. Make sure that you know what you are doing every morning that you wake up to avoid repeating the previous mistakes day in and day out.

In conclusion you should not let your day be ruined by what you did not do yesterday or what you want to do tomorrow. Instead you should live every day as it comes. Start every morning with all your energy paying attention to the things you want to achieve.

Where To Look For Inspiration

> Over recent years my morning routine has become more tight and focused. *The older I get, the less time I want to waste.*
>
> – Mars Dorian
>
> Photo via skitterphoto.com

At times we just need some little inspiration to forge ahead.

This depends with what inspires you most. Some people listen to their favorite songs and others read motivational quotations or watch inspiring video clips. A little motivation can give you the encouragement or drive that you need for the day. Apart from these inspirational resources, you can check out anything that helps you focus on your day to day chores. This should be done early in the morning before you kick start your work day.

Decide what is more important.

Think of the most important things that you want to achieve on that day and get what you require to achieve your objectives right away. Success is not something that you own; it's all about what you do so you can move from one social class to another. Success is something that you may experience after a long day of hard work. Keep in mind that today is special and will never be around again. With this in mind, make those important calls in the morning to ensure that you have all the resources that you need to make your day more successful.

Important Things That You Need To Learn About Morning Routines

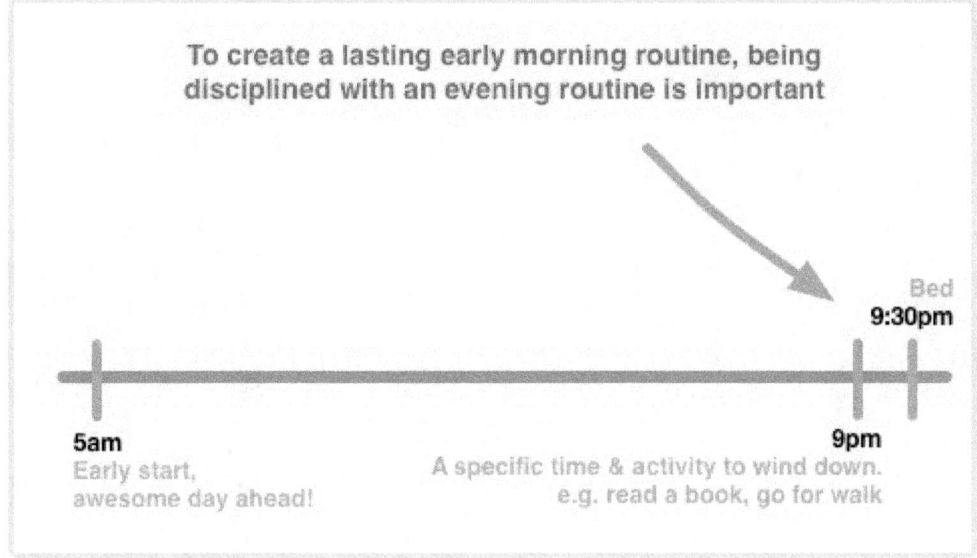

To create a lasting early morning routine, being disciplined with an evening routine is important

Bed
9:30pm

5am
Early start,
awesome day ahead!

9pm
A specific time & activity to wind down.
e.g. read a book, go for walk

Draft a Morning Ritual

If you check out the morning rituals of the rich and famous then you will discover that they have a strict morning routine that they repeat 6 – 7 days a week. A ritual is a schedule that you choose to follow invariably for a period of time with the intention of keeping it as consistent and regular as possible.

All you need to do right now is figure out what you need to do in the morning and then repeat the same to achieve success. Wake up early, grab a glass of lemon water, take in a 10 minute walk on the treadmill, make some lemon juice and then leave your house.

Take a Good Breakfast

Ever heard that breakfast is the most important meal of the day? That is 100% true. Without eating a healthy breakfast, your body will be operating on fumes until lunch time when you will be so hungry to take any unhealthy meal that comes your way. Eating a healthy breakfast will equip your body with the resources it needs to keep going.

The best thing to do is to rise early so that you can have enough time to prepare a healthy breakfast. A wholesome breakfast is what you need to have a fast and easily healthy day. Furthermore, taking your breakfast at home is much more fulfilling than carrying your coffee cup to work.

Stretching and Exercising

A few pushups and 10 minutes of walking can keep you healthy by refreshing your blood, pumping it right as you get ready to set yourself up for the day ahead. Of course, there are other perfect times that you can exercise but morning hours should never be canceled. Morning exercise keeps you on the right foot as you will come away from it with the right energy and feeling refreshed.

Reflect and Strategize

Have you already set your goals? Right! There is no better time to review your goals and plans than early in the morning. After studying a number of things that the rich do in the morning, it has been found that 50% of the most successful people out there spare a few minutes to read the scriptures for spiritual nourishment and plan for the day ahead. This gives them the confidence they require to push ahead.

How To Keep A Successful Morning Routine

Creating a successful morning routine is much easier than maintaining it. First, you must be ready to do what successful people do from the time they wake up to the time they start working. If you can learn all about what the rich do in the morning then you are on the right path towards finding out exactly what you should be doing to become a successful person. Make your morning routine a habit and you will not have any problems starting your days perfectly. You can find the best morning routines by examining what you have been doing every morning and knowing the new routines that you must adopt to make them more perfect.

Conclusion

As you have learned in this guide, you have everything that you need to know about successful morning routines, including the benefits of waking up early in the morning, the things that you need to tie into your morning routines, how to design a perfect morning routine and the common pitfalls that you should avoid if you want to follow the right path towards getting all you have ever desired in life. You should not lose hope if you are not able to get started right away, because not all people are morning persons.

The whole idea of waking up early in the morning and scheduling your morning routine like the rich can at times fail but that should not discourage you from achieving your dreams. Our advice is for you to start small by designing your morning routine with the simple things that you feel you can achieve and then expand your to do list as time goes by. This way you will not end up stressed if you are not able to achieve all the things you had included in your morning routine.

As it has been mentioned earlier, a well-executed routine in the morning can help you realize more success than any other thing that you do in the course of the day. Your motivation levels are high in the morning and this is the best time for you to give your best to your new projects and some social attachments.

This book will help learn all the productive things that you need to do immediately after waking up. Great morning routines also set a productive tone for the remaining part of the day. You should not feel discouraged if you fail to do what you wanted in the morning because you have the rest of the day to achieve your morning goals.

Back Cover Description For The Book

This morning routine book covers in detail what the rich/wealthy/famous in the world people do immediately after they wake up to make their morning hours more successful. Given that every person has different interests and hobbies, this book covers everything that you can do in the morning for a productive and positive day. This book focuses on all the things that you should include in your morning routine. All the things that you can do in the morning have been well explained so that you can understand what you need to do to achieve your dreams. After understanding what you need to do in the morning, the book gives an in-depth analysis of everything that you need to do in the morning. This great book is an excellent choice for those looking to do like the wealthy and famous do immediately when they wake up. All the morning routines discussed in this book are easy to design and follow, thus making it a highly recommended book for anyone who wants to become successful by doing what is right in the morning.